Nature's Children

GIBBONS

WITHDRAWN

Ben Hoare

GROLIER

FACTS IN BRIEF

Classification of Gibbons

Class:	*Mammalia* (mammals)
Order:	*Primates* (primates)
Family:	*Hylobatidae* (gibbons)
Genus:	*Hylobates*
Species:	There are 11 species of gibbons.

World distribution. Throughout Southeast Asia from southern China and the eastern part of India south as far as Indonesia.

Habitat. The highest layers of tropical rain forests.

Distinctive physical characteristics. Slender body, small head, very long arms and legs, nimble hands, thick coat of shaggy fur, bare face, and no tail.

Habits. Seldom leave the treetops. Swing from branch to branch at great speed. Live in small family groups. Call and sing loudly to each other.

Diet. Mainly fruit; also leaves, flowers, seeds, insects, spiders, and birds' eggs.

© 2004 The Brown Reference Group plc
Printed and bound in U.S.A.
Edited by John Farndon and Angela Koo

Published by:

GROLIER

An imprint of Scholastic Library Publishing Old Sherman Turnpike, Danbury, Connecticut 06816

Library of Congress Cataloging-in-Publication Data

Hoare, Ben.
    Gibbons / Ben Hoare.
        p. cm. — (Nature's children)
    Includes index.
    Summary: Describes the physical characteristics, behavior, and habitats of gibbons.
    ISBN 0–7172–5957–9 (set)   ISBN 0–7172–5965–X
    1. Gibbons—Juvenile literature. [1. Gibbons.] I. Title. II. Series.

QL737.P96H57 2004
599.88′2—dc21

2003049169

Contents

A dark shape crashes through the treetops. It's moving so fast that you get only brief glimpses of its long arms and shaggy fur. Suddenly it leaps across a large gap between two trees. Moments later it vanishes into the forest.

This mysterious creature was a gibbon. Gibbons are completely at home in the tallest trees. They climb and swing far above the ground as easily as you and I stroll along the sidewalk. They sleep, feed, mate, and give birth high among the branches.

Gibbons are special for lots of other reasons, too. They live in families as we do, and early each morning the mother and father gibbon sing to each other. They are among the noisiest apes in the whole forest!

With eyes facing forward like ours, gibbons have amazingly expressive faces. You can almost imagine what this lar gibbon is thinking.

Kings of the Swingers

Gibbons move in a spectacular way. Instead of running up and down branches, these animals swing underneath them. They reach out with first one arm then the other—left, right, left, right. Sometimes gibbons hurtle from branch to branch until the trees flash by. They seem almost to be flying through the forest. If need be, gibbons can swing along faster than an Olympic sprinter can run.

The acrobatic skill of gibbons is breath-taking. They can jump 30 feet (9 meters) from one tree to the next. One of their tricks is to hang from a branch by one arm and use the other to pick fruit—their favorite food.

Gibbons swing through the trees with their arms with tremendous speed and agility.

Amazing Acrobats

What makes a gibbon such a superb acrobat? The answer is simple—its skeleton. Its bones are light, and it has a slim body. That saves lots of weight. The lighter, the better! The gibbon's arms are also incredibly long. If the gibbon stands up, its hands drag on the ground. That is a nuisance on the ground but really useful in the trees. Long arms allow the gibbon to grab branches farther away. They also give it more momentum as it swings along through the trees.

A gibbon's fingers and toes are long and strong. It uses them to hook onto branches. The gibbon also has special shoulder joints so it can twist its arms in any direction. When the gibbon hangs under a branch, it can rotate its body in a circle without letting go. You or I would fall off if we tried that!

A gibbon owes its acrobatic flair to its long fingers and long arms that can bend and twist almost any way.

Great Apes and Lesser Apes

Opposite page:
No creature in the world is more like us than the chimpanzee— clever with its fingers, intelligent, and very sociable and expressive.

Gibbons belong to a group of mammals called apes. They are the smallest apes, so are known as the lesser apes. The other apes include orangutans, chimpanzees, gorillas, and humans. They are known as the great apes. All apes can stand upright and walk on two legs. They are highly intelligent and have nimble hands that can handle objects. Apes are related to monkeys; but unlike monkeys, they have no tail.

Great apes often visit the ground. In fact, mountain gorillas hardly ever climb trees. But gibbons spend nearly their whole lives up trees. They are more agile than other apes because they are smaller and lighter. Most gibbons weigh only 12–16 pounds (5.5–7.25 kilograms). A big male gorilla may be up to 30 times heavier than a gibbon!

Gibbons like this lar gibbon live so high in the trees that they can easily find a spot in the sun.

Where in the World?

Gibbons live in the lush green forests of Southeast Asia. They range over a vast area stretching from southern China to the island of Java, which lies in the Indian Ocean between Asia and Australia. There are gibbons as far west as India and as far east as Vietnam.

The climate in this part of the world is hot and wet. It rains so much that the forests are called rain forests. The frequent downpours and high temperatures help all kinds of plants grow. Some of the trees have massive trunks that soar to 165 feet (50 meters). The tops of the trees link up to make a platform of branches and leaves known as the forest canopy. Up here it is sunny, and there's plenty of food for gibbons to eat. This is the part of the forest gibbons like best.

The Gibbon Family

Scientists group gibbons together in the same family because these animals are alike in many ways. The gibbon family's scientific name is Hylobatidae (said HIGH-low-bat-e-die). It means "tree walker." There are 11 different types, or species, of gibbons. Some of them look so similar that they are difficult to tell apart. It is likely that there are more species of gibbons, but people have not yet learned how to identify them.

Each kind of gibbon lives in a different part of Southeast Asia. Some gibbons range across a wide area. Others survive in just a few places. The islands of Java, Borneo, and Mentawai all have their own variety of gibbon that is not found anywhere else.

With its white eyebrows and little goatee beard, the rare Javan, or silvery, gibbon is easy to tell from its more common cousins.

Like all apes, gibbons have no hair around their eyes and nose. The lar gibbon's face is fringed with white fur.

Colorful Fur

Gibbons are covered with shaggy fur on most of their body, except for their fingers, palms, and the soles of their feet. The hair is also shorter on the face. The most colorful gibbon is the siamang. Its fur may be black, brown, reddish, cream, white, or multicolored. White-checked gibbons and golden-cheeked gibbons are named for the bright patches on their cheeks. Lar, or white-handed, gibbons have white hands and feet, and dark faces with a fringe of pale hairs around the edge.

Newborn gibbons are almost hairless apart from a furry cap on the head. They soon develop a coat of silvery, yellow, or whitish fur. Their fur usually gets darker as they grow older. Male and female gibbons may be different colors, but they are roughly the same size and shape.

Sticking Together

It is fairly unusual to see a gibbon on its own. A gibbon might appear to be alone, but there will probably be others nearby. Gibbons like company, and they live in small family groups. Each family includes an adult male and female plus several of their offspring. Most families have two or three young of various ages. There might be a baby, a youngster under five years old, and perhaps an older brother or sister or two.

Gibbons reach adult size at around seven or eight years of age. At this stage of their lives they are the gibbon equivalent of teenagers. In the wild, gibbons live up to 30 years or so. In captivity some gibbons have managed to live more than 40 years.

Home Sweet Home

A gibbon family stays in the same patch of forest all year round. This area is the family's territory. It is the size of 50–100 football fields, and it provides the gibbons with everything they need. Hundreds of different trees and plants grow in the territory. They produce fruit at different times, so there is always enough to eat.

Gibbons patrol their territory regularly. Over the years they get to know it extremely well. They know where all the local fruit trees are. They learn every shortcut through the treetops and know the best places to hide. Wild gibbons can be very hard to spot. You could spend several days in a rain forest and not see a single gibbon.

Dawn Chorus

At daybreak, soon after the gibbon family wakes up, the mother begins to sing. Hers is a strange and ghostly sound. The female hoots, howls, trills, and wails. She sings slowly at first, but gets faster and louder. Then she stops and starts all over again. The father joins in, and the two gibbons perform a long duet. The youngsters often sing along with their parents.

Gibbons sing for around 30 minutes most mornings. No one knows for sure why they do it. The female probably sings to tell other gibbons nearby that this is her bit of the forest. It is her way of saying, "Keep off my backyard." The parents might also sing to strengthen the friendship between them.

Every gibbon sounds slightly different. With practice scientists can recognize individual gibbons from just their voices.

Opposite page:
The howling of mother gibbons in the early morning air is one of the most thrilling sounds in the jungle. The sound carries for up to a mile (1.6 kilometers).

Border Wars

Opposite page:
Gibbons are not always friendly to each other. When neighboring families meet, they make a lot of loud noise, whooping and growling.

Neighboring gibbon families often bump into each other where their two territories meet. When this happens, noisy squabbles break out. The gibbons rush forward to get a good look at the other family. They whoop and growl angrily. All the older gibbons join in.

Sometimes there is a battle between the adult male from each family. The rivals chase one another up, down, and around the trees at top speed. They rush back and forth, hooting loudly. A gibbon may even bite his opponent's leg or arm during the chase.

The dispute may last only a few minutes or go on for up to an hour. After a while the noise dies down. The gibbons retreat to their own separate areas of the forest, and peace returns once more.

Fruits of the Forest

Gibbons eat mainly fruit. They are particularly fond of figs and wild mangoes. When a family of gibbons finds a big tree covered with ripe fruit, they get very excited. Other animals arrive to join the feast, including colorful parrots, green pigeons, squirrels, monkeys, and hornbills. Hornbills are large birds that use their huge beaks to pluck fruit and swallow it whole. There may be quite a party in the tree!

Gibbons move right out to the tips of the thinnest branches. That is where the juiciest fruit grows. They also feed on leaves, flowers, tender shoots, and seeds. Occasionally they eat insects and spiders or steal eggs from birds' nests. But these things make up only a small part of their diet.

What gibbons like to eat more than anything is fruit. When they find a fruit tree, all the family leaps in and starts munching furiously.

Leaf Eater

The siamang eats less fruit than other gibbons. Instead, it prefers leaves. It chooses only fresh, green leaves. It is very fussy about which trees it feeds in. The siamang knows which leaves taste good and ignores altogether the ones that taste awful.

The siamang is the largest and heaviest kind of gibbon. Unlike other gibbons, it has a special pouch under its chin. The siamang blows air into this pouch like a balloon until it is as big as its head. With the pouch fully inflated, the siamang is able to call much louder. It is the loudest of all the gibbons— its booming calls can be heard 2 miles (3 kilometers) away.

Siamangs are the biggest gibbons. They have a huge balloonlike bag under their chin to make sure they have the biggest voices, too!

It's late morning, it's hot, and it's time for the gibbons to stretch out for their daily nap.

The High Life

Most days gibbons follow a similar routine. After singing together at dawn, the family spends a few hours looking for food. In late morning, when it starts to get hot, the gibbons rest a while. They pass the time by snoozing in the sun or by cleaning their fur. Cleaning, or grooming, is a group activity. The gibbons take turns combing through each other's fur with their long fingers. They remove dirt and any little critters they find.

In midafternoon the family sets off again in search of food. Normally the adults lead the way, with the young following behind. On a typical day they might travel around one mile (1.6 kilometers). But during the rainy season the gibbons often have to take shelter. They huddle among thick foliage to avoid getting soaked. Sometimes it pours with rain for hours, and they hardly move all day.

Down to Earth

Opposite page:
Gibbons can walk on the ground on two legs, but they don't find it easy. They have to throw their arms out to balance.

Gibbons seldom come down to the ground. They can even get a drink without leaving the trees. The gibbons dip their hands into a hole in a tree trunk filled with rainwater. Often they simply rub their hands against wet leaves, then suck their damp fur. But there are times when gibbons must visit the forest floor. For example, they might need to cross a clearing in the forest. Young gibbons sometimes have to walk between two trees if the gap is too large for them to jump across.

On the ground gibbons walk and hop on their back legs. They hold their arms out to help them balance like tightrope walkers. It is hard work—their gangly legs are suited to swinging through trees, not walking. Gibbons cannot swim, and they avoid water.

Time for Bed

When it starts to get dark, the gibbons choose somewhere safe to sleep for the night. The family has several favorite sleeping trees in their territory. They pick giant trees that give a good view over the surrounding forest.

Gibbons differ from other apes because they don't make nests to sleep in. Chimps, gorillas, and orangutans make a new nest every night. They bend back several branches to create a cosy hammock. Gibbons sleep sitting upright on a wide branch or in the fork between two branches. This is more comfortable than it sounds. Gibbons have tough, leathery pads on their backsides that act like cushions!

As the sun goes down, a lar gibbon finds a nice, comfortable spot high in the trees. It bends back a branch or two for extra comfort and puts its head down for a nice sleep.

Danger in the Night

Few animals are fast enough to catch and eat gibbons. Gibbons have excellent hearing and sharp eyesight. As soon as a gibbon senses danger, it calls to alert the others. If the enemy gets too close, the gibbons quickly disappear into the branches.

Gibbons are most at risk from predators at night. Leopards prowl through the rain forest in the darkness, and they often climb trees to hunt sleeping birds and mammals. A leopard can easily kill an adult gibbon. The other main enemies of gibbons are big snakes such as pythons. Pythons also hunt at night. They detect prey with their acute sense of smell. A python kills its prey by wrapping tight coils around the animals' bodies. Eventually its unlucky victims cannot breathe at all, and they die from lack of air.

*Even high in the treetops a gibbon is not always
safe from a leopard prowling through the night.*

Faithful Friends

When a male and female gibbon start a family, they usually stay together for the rest of their lives. Their friendship is very strong. Every day they sing together and groom each other. The male gibbon guards his partner closely. He does not allow other adult males to come anywhere near her. The female, too, chases away adult females that approach her partner.

A female gibbon can breed at any time of year. She has her first baby when she is around nine years old. The female is pregnant for around seven months. She gives birth to a single baby high up in the trees. It is extremely rare for a gibbon to have twins.

Male and female gibbons form very strong and affectionate partnerships, like this pair of siamang gibbons.

New Baby

A newborn baby gibbon weighs only 6 ounces (170 grams)—less than a cup of water. Although it is helpless, the tiny infant can cling tightly to its mother's fur. When mom swings through the treetops, she lifts up her legs to give her baby extra support and protection. When the mother gibbon is resting, she raises her knees to form a snug cradle for the baby to sleep in.

After a few weeks the baby starts to clamber around the female's body. The other members of the family take a great interest in the new arrival. But mom is fiercely protective of her offspring, and she pushes the others away if they pester her too much.

Like a human baby, a baby gibbon needs a lot of care and attention. For the first year of its life it clings tightly onto mom—and mom won't let her baby out of sight for an instant.

Growing Up

The baby gibbon grows fast. Early on it learns to steal food from mom's hand. Sometimes it tries to copy her and reaches out to pick fruit off a branch. But the youngster is too clumsy and generally drops it! When the gibbon is around one year old, it is more agile and starts to move through the trees on its own. But mom gathers it up at the first sign of danger.

Gradually the young gibbon learns how to swing from tree to tree properly and how to find ripe fruit. Singing takes a little longer to master. Within two and a half or three years the gibbon can look after itself. Now its parents are ready to have another baby.

Young gibbons remain with their family until fully grown. Then they leave to join another family or start a new one of their own.

Opposite page:
By the time it's about a year old, a young gibbon is starting to play around in the forest by itself. It tries out its swinging technique safe on the ground. But mom is never far away.

Gibbons in Danger

Opposite page:
Nowadays, seeing a hoolock, or white-browed, gibbon swinging through the trees is a rare sight. Their forest home has been so reduced that there are now very few hoolocks left.

Today gibbons are much less common than they used to be. Scientists worry that the Javan gibbon, black gibbon, and hoolock, or white-browed gibbon, might even die out, or go extinct. Gibbons are getting rare because they face many different threats. The most serious threat is the loss of their habitat—the forests where they live. Vast areas of rain forest in Southeast Asia have been cut down to provide timber. People also burn and clear forest to use the land for farming. Gibbons need large forests, and they cannot always survive in the small pieces of forest that remain.

Every year many gibbons are caught alive to be sold as pets. Hunters kill thousands more gibbons for food. People also hunt gibbons for their bones and body parts, which are used in traditional medicine. Some local people believe that powder made from gibbon bones can cure stiffness and bad backs.

Saving Gibbons

Lots of things can be done to help save gibbons. Large parts of forest in countries such as Thailand, Malaysia, and Indonesia are now national parks. In these areas the forest is protected by law. There are rules that limit how many trees can be cut down for timber. Rangers patrol the parks to stop the hunters.

Gibbons are wonderful animals and are delightful to watch. If people knew more about them, they might want to help protect them. Gibbons are apes just as we are. They deserve looking after for future generations to enjoy.

Words to Know

Apes A group of mammals that includes gibbons, orangutans, chimpanzees, gorillas, and humans.

Canopy The highest part of a forest, where branches at the top of neighboring trees touch each other.

Duet When two animals sing together, each with its own part.

Extinct When all of the animals of a particular species have died, and there are no more left anywhere in the world.

Foliage Mass of branches, twigs, and leaves on a tree or bush.

Grooming When two mammals use their fingers or teeth as combs to clean each other's fur.

Habitat The type of place an animal lives in, such as forest or desert.

Mammal Typically hairy, warm-blooded animal that gives birth to live young and produces milk to feed them.

Mating When a male and female animal come together to produce young.

Predator An animal that hunts and eats other animals for food.

Prey An animal that is hunted and eaten by a predator.

Rain forest A usually tropical forest with lots of tall trees where it rains frequently.

Species A particular type of animal or plant.

INDEX

Cover Photo: NHPA: E. A. Janes
Photo Credits: Ardea: 37, Kenneth W. Fink 15, Andrea Florence 12, Uwe Florence 7, Adrian
Warren 11, M. Watson 30; Bruce Coleman: Gerald S. Cubitt 42, Werner Layer 22, Uwe Walz
4; NHPA: Joe Blossom 26, 41, Mark Bowler 25, Martin Harvey 8, 34, Dave Watts 20/21, 33;
Oxford Scientific Films: Dick Michael/AA 38, Dinodia Picture Agency 45, Stan Osolinski 29,
Alistair Shay 16.